Brown Blossoms
Healing Poemstories

ALVIN HERRING

Poemstories for a Loved People

ALEXHON PRESS

Copyright © 1995 Alexhon Press
Reprinted 1999

ISBN 0-9645151-0-5

Library of Congress Catalogue Card Number: 94-80268

Edited and designed by the
Alexhon Press Division of
© Alexhon Electronic Publishing, LLC
P.O. Box 17531
Arlington, VA 22216

Copy Editor: Winnifred Levy
Design and Typsetting: Kerri Washington
Photography: Images by Saul

Typset in Palatino and Katfish
Printed in the United States

Alexhon Press books are available at special discounts for bulk
purchases for sales promotions, premiums, fund-raising, or
educational use.

Dedication

to my sons Brandon and Ryan –
"remember there is strength in tears"

To Pamela,

God Bless you
& you sweetheart!
Powerful leadership

Love
Ro Al

Table Of Contents

My Home

Acknowledgement

This book is dedicated to Ruth and Alvin Herring Jr., my mother and father. Each gave me so much and asked so little in return. I also dedicate this book to my wife Deborah and my sons Brandon and Ryan. Without their love, patience and encouragement this book would have never been written. Love and gratitude are given to my sister Cassandra and my brother David. They have always been my heroes. And a special appreciation to all of my loving friends, particularly Bob, Barry and Cherrie. Their love and gentle nudging ensured the completion of this book.

And a final dedication is to the Ancestors. This book is testimony to the constant presence of love and hope in my life that I know is a gift from those who have gone before me. I hope that what I have written reflects my gratitude to all who have given me guidance, and I hope gives honor to their legacy. ◈

Foreward

I am overjoyed to have had the opportunity to write this book. The ideas, dreams, thoughts, questions that it represents have been swimming in my head for such a long time. I am relieved that they are finally out and on paper. It is as if these poems have been forming in my head since my birth, and I needed to nurture them and watch them grow until I could trust that they would tell my story – our story – in the way I needed to tell it. I trust these words. They have a truth to them that I am proud of. They have a familiarity to them that you will recognize.

It's been said that all poetry is autobiographical. Some deny it, but you'll get no denials from me. These pages speak my truths. I have known loss, pain, sorrow and death. I have felt the alienation of racism, and have had my bouts with rage. I know too well the search for significance and the fear of failure. I know the desperation that comes with thinking too long about being free. And I know the saving mercy of an unseen God and the beauty of a resurrected life.

My hope is that these things that I have felt, you too have felt. And that in the telling of my story, I tell a piece of yours as well. Writing this book reminded me of the obligation that we have to share our lives with each other, to offer our experience to each other and to give to each other that which we cherish dearly – our memories and our desires. As African people we desperately need to be with each other during these current times. These times demand that we renew our bonds of love and tell and re-tell the ancestral stories of hope, triumph and pride. We need a village full of griots who can pass on the words that will remind us of our importance to ourselves and to the universe.

To that end I offer this collection of poems. They are more like stories really, that re-tell the journey from our ancestral homeland, across the oceans of the diaspora to the shores of our present existence. I hope what I've written will be helpful and useful to you. I hope above all else that this work will encourage you to smile, to cry and to heal. ◈

A Prayer

Dear Lord, in the presence of the ancestors bless the reading of this book. Allow these words their own voice, their own time, their own life. Permit these words to guide, teach and to heal. And above all else Most Sacred One, permit these words to advance your love within me and within my people. Humbly and respectfully, I offer this prayer on behalf of all of the children of the diaspora. ◈

Home

...and the mighty people walked
like gods upon the shore

I am an African. This is the truest statement of identity I can utter. To say that I am American first is like beginning a book in the middle of its pages. In the beginning, there was only Africa. And it is there...on that soil that all life began, that I began...

African Man

I wound the clock of time
I swam the original waters
I was mate to the first woman
and father to the children of all time
it was I who first tasted the sun upon my body
and it was I who planted the plenty by moonlight

I am the first ancestor
and it is my spirit that speaks to you in a voice that you
can only hear when your heart stills
it is my blood that runs through all of you
it is my spirit that gives you wings

I AM YOUR FATHER
father to all villages

I AM YOUR MATE
I choose you

I AM YOUR BROTHER
I run by your side

I AM YOUR SON
I sit at your table on your right

I do not hide my greatness
or deny my importance
I am beholding to none of God's creatures

I AM WHOLE AND INDIVISIBLE by any thought or deed
that might choose to come against me

I AM STRONG – filled with natural courage
I can not bend
nor can I retreat

I AM AN AFRICAN MAN

and God was pleased with me when I was born ◈

African Woman

I am the beginning

The Most Sacred One ripped a hole in the heavens
and with great cause pulled me from a place of perfection
and brought me to this place
and brought me to this task
to mother a planet of people
and set the pendulum of life in motion
I have taken to this task with consummate joy
and I have done it well

I was well suited for this role
for it has been said that I am powerful

and this is so

for **only I** could convince the earth to place its bounty in my hands
only I could make the sky bend down to shelter my children
only I could seduce the winds to blow gently and with kindness
only I could fill the world with motherlove and sisterlove
and lose them to find and fill every open space
and **only I** could walk beside **African Man**
I do not own him but he reveres me
I am in every way his equal and he knows that

I AM AFRICAN WOMAN

I am **first** woman
therefore I am the mother in your heart
the sister by your side

the wife who shares your bed
and the daughter
who offers tender affection at your feet

I AM AFRICAN WOMAN

and that means I am perfection wrapped in an ebony
skinned robe of splendor ◈

Africa...The Righteous Land

deep
rich
fertile
ancient
eternal
universal
Godknown
home

The Righteous Land

love colored
vital
musical
passion-hearted
spirit rich
timeless
ancestor-led

This Righteous Land

reach across the space that grief and hurt created
and plunge into the eyes of your people
eyes that ask beyond words

did you know me as a child

did you know how I was carried in the womb

how I was given to people

and who I was given to

how I have made my ripples upon this great
                                                    sea

Africa is calling you to reach to each other
reach and call out brother
reach and call out sister
reach with the knowledge that the universe will embrace your
reaching
and you will be delivered to each other and given to love in every way

so hold onto each other

        tighter still

and let your hands bring a healing touch
you will not find a better way to make your walk
than to make it together

        all the way

to the beloved Righteous Land ◈

how hot is the Saharan sun?
how long is the Sarangethi day?
how deep are the waters of the Nile?
and over how many mountains does a cloud glide on its way from
Isle Goree to Kenyan Savanna?

where does the regal elephant bathe at noon?
where is the freespace for the cheetah to run beyond the speed
of wild and savage?
how many egrets stretch from Congo sun-up
to Zimbabwean sun-down?
and how many frozen tears of African joy crown Mount Kilamanjaro?

these now are the questions that ply the conscious waters of so many
Black souls

we may not know the answers
but we have not forgotten the magic
in the question ❖

I Dreamed Of The Gambia

it is some boat
carved out of a tree
its insides are rough
and it rides low in the water

he does not talk
he's strong in his distance
he looks from riverbank to riverbank
never blinking

there is the constant sound of birds not visible
they talk among themselves about my coming
they know the truth

it smells mud-wet
it is thick and nearly burst its banks
slow but not tame
it knows where I'm going

it is slipping now
hanging low
hanging on
it has not given up on me

she closes in from all sides
she is opaque
she reveals nothing
...and she causes me to shudder

and I can only dream of the Gambia ◈

African Essence

when I was in Lagos
I went into a small jewelry shop
and there among the diamonds and rubies
I saw a woman-child
she was cloaked in a flowing kente
that fluttered on the breeze
making her appear angelic
azure wings of fine cloth
seemed to lift her from the ground
as she passed me

she did not speak
and I could not speak...
her beauty captured all of my words

her African essence was the most brilliant jewel of all ◈

Father Africa

(for Nelson Mandela)

My father Africa
of what do you dream
lying there within your cold prison cell?

do you dream of freedom?
borne on the synchronized chants of a million Black warriors
standing proud in the Natal sun
their hearts pregnant with anticipation of your call to battle
spear and shield poised
ready to carry out the order of the day

do you dream of rising up like waves of heat
from the floor of your verdant homeland
      shimmering
         moving like a storm

              rising up in spirit
                 rising up in spirit
                    rising up
to wrest the power from hands
foreign to your heart

do you dream of a mighty conference
men and women of all colors
seated around
your table
carved from the tree of peace
where words are called to do the fighting
and tears to do the peacemaking

or do you dream of your brown-skinned bride
eyes of ebony and alabaster
bosom of warmth and comfort
and round-faced children with unashamed laughter
and unfettered joy

and you

father Africa

seated in your old chair in the doorway of your big house
with yet another grandchild cradled in your unshackled arms

of what do you dream father Africa

I wonder this aloud
for you have been asleep in my heart
oh these many years ◈

When A Black Man Dreams Of Africa

(for Langston)

what happens when you have a dream
of something grand you have not seen
does it exist as some mirage
or does it come to warn?

and if it tends to linger on
and comes up daily as the dawn
does it exist as real things do
or is it mere suspicion?

and if it lifts the veil of night
and occupies the slumber's rite
can we say it is alive
or still a fascination?

but when it clouds the conscious thought
and becomes the gift that longings brought
it must be then that we call it truth
more than a passing inspiration

...I am possessed by such a dream of Africa ◆

Mother Africa

Mother...Mother Africa
bring me close
let me suckle at your breast
touch me gently...and call me son

Mother...Mother Africa
I'm hurt Mother
        I'm hurt bad...
rock me slowly Mother
...............sing to me low

Mother...Mother Africa
teach me how to cry
teach me how to heal myself
...........let me cry Mother.............cry for me

Mother...Mother Africa hold my hands
...........don't let me hurt myself anymore
..............................forgive me Mother...........make God forgive me
show me how to forgive myself

Mother...Mother Africa
put your old arms around me
......let me close Mother
so I can smell your ancient body
.....let me caress your wrinkled face
.....let me kiss your eyes
..............I need to know you after all these centuries
so just let me sit with you....Mother.....and touch you
.......and know you're real

Mother ... Mother Africa
let me just rest my head on your lap

stroke my brow Mother and tell me **my** story
tell me about **my** kinfolk
........give me **my** ancestors Mother
so I might know I'm not ever alone

Mother...Mother Africa
hold me up
help me stand
place your warm hand on my back....steady me Mother
............you showed me how to walk once Mother....a long time ago
....show me now
........show me my path Mother and push me gently out
...............out into this world that moves around and through me

In return for all of this Mother Africa...

I will live and give life
I will love as you command
I will seek out and worship our God
I will remember the ancestors
I will love my kin and practice peace with those whose life I touch

and most of all....Mother Africa

I will see you in all that I do
....in all that I believe
....in all that I love

I pledge all this knowing that it will please you
...and even then it will be but a drop in the ocean of love that swells
from your heart for me

I have been Mothered well ◈

The Mighty People

One day
tucked inside the eon-plenty cloak of time
they appeared
and...

they walked upon the glassy waters
of a sea that calmed at their command
their skin, brilliant in that primordial day, glistened
as they strode so sure and tall
beads of water dotted their brow and rolled slowly
down their necks
and along the lines of their arms
and dripped from their fingertips

the sun tasted generously of their beautiful bodies
and so pleased was it to find such perfect canvasses for its art
that it painted them with its richest browns
and ebonies
and bronzes
and golds

the birds played joyfully overhead
winging on sea-wind
gliding carelessly along
so awed were they by the sight of the **mighty people**
that their words of praise were forever changed to song
and they have been singing of them since

all the creatures of the sea followed on their heels
parting the waters with their frenetic dances of jubilation
creating a powerful wave that washed all the waters back
and revealing the ocean floor as a jeweled carpet

the air stood still

      the heavens broke into a wide sea-blue smile

and the **mighty people**

      in all their splendor

walked like Gods upon the shore ◈

How I Found Myself

the spirit of
African ancestors
blew in
the moment
I
opened
a window
to my
soul ◈

Home Lost

...think for a moment, how did
you come to these shores?

My father was born the son of a sharecropper...My grandfather was born the son of a sharecropper too...My great-grandfather was born a slave...

Manchild's Last Day

on my last day of freedom...

I awoke from a child's sleep
and leaped from my dreams
into my mother's waiting brown arms

her skin was soft against my cheek
she had the sweet smell of mother's milk
she spoke my name and without hesitation
my mouth convulsed into a broad smile

this was love
I knew it was real

I heard my father's voice above those of my uncles
his was the proud voice
he was a powerful man
a warrior man
yet as I approached him the corners of his eyes softened
he greeted me with a gentle kiss atop my head
the spot where his lips landed was the same spot
each time he kissed me
this is my father's spot I thought
how glad I was to yield this spot to him

...this was love
and I knew it was real

the men were about to go on a hunt
my mother called me back to get the
amulet that she made me wear
every time I hunted with the men
It blessed me she said

I wheeled on my heals to wave her a goodbye

and what happened next I can only describe
as the end of my human existence...

there are no words that can show you where the pain
of that moment resides in my heart

the slavers were quick in their savagery
the brutality of their attack mesmerized me
I was stuck
I couldn't move
things were whirling in my head
everything seemed to be spinning about me
in every direction
blood flowed freely mingling with moans and shouts
and hastily made prayers to the war gods
urine ran down my ashy trembling legs
my mouth was dry
I could hardly breath
and my heart beat with an insistence
that it be set free of my body and the pain of that
horrible moment

...my mother fell hard
I watched her fall
the amulet dangling from her bloodied hand
its last blessing was a gift of quick death

my uncles fought in a way that I can only describe
as vicious
like animals

they instinctively fought for the center of the clearing
broad backs touching
arms flailing
this is how they told me they would fight
if the slavers came to our village
they killed many men that day
– before they fell –
and I can bear witness to that

...my father's knife was a bloody blur
as it worked within the heaving mass
of men at war
he fought his way free
and for a moment I thought he might escape the attack
and swoop me up into the safety of his arms
but within the space of an eyeblink his life
was given back to the Gods

and his knife fell to the ground
its blade tip hauntingly pointing at me

I can not tell you what happened next
I do not know
but I am bound head and foot by lacerating iron chains
and I am kept in darkness
my captors despise me
my wretchedness consumes my ebbing energy

the only solace is my remembrance
that I was loved once
and it was real

it was real? ◈

How Slaves Lived And Died

heads bent...
from crouching in low places
eyes black...
from not being able to cry tears of known
sadness and familiar terror
only tears of horrid and invincible fear

skin ashen...
dull
not brilliant at all
but more shroud-like
like a sack holding together a loose collection of
spent human artifacts

hearts rent through
leaking from every valve and artery
the precious fluid of emotional sanity
and uncomplicated love

souls...
so heavy they can be seen plainly by the eye
no longer ethereal
but brought by pain into the known world
a place too harsh

too sinister

slaves were born
they lived
they died

and they beg us now to make sense of our lives ◈

Meditation

think for a moment...
how did you come to these shores?

did you come as a baby-child
tucked like a seed inside the womb
of some frightened bride...
did she know you were there?
did she know what was waiting for you on this side?

did you come as an old woman
too tired to fight,
wanting desperately the comfort of grandchildren
and the shade of a spreading baobab tree?
when did you cry those tears that said,
"I'll never see my home again?"

did you come as an angry man-child,
reaching manhood, like Jonah, inside the belly
of some slave ship?
were you old enough to understand that you would never know
freedom as a man?

did you come as a revered Oba?
king in your land...
a god possessing the power to give dance and song and joy?
how did you hide your shame
when they called on you for deliverance
and you could deliver nothing?

did you come as a young princess from a land of grand villages...
from a family that had many cattle

and a family name that brought smiles of love
to those that spoke it?
were you able to hide your beauty from the slavers
or did they take that too?

ask yourself, "how did you come to these shores?"

why did they endure so much
see so much
hurt so much for us
and yet live?
were they saying to us through their sacrifice
that life has a precious mystery?
were they saying, "go find the joy?"
did they know we would get so lost...
be so afraid of life?
did they fight so to stay alive in
our dreams
our prayers...
our very cells
so that we might call on them
as we do now
to lead us back home? ❖

The Children That Slavery Killed

oh how they must have cried when we were gone...

the sadness must have been more than their little hearts
could bear
surely they must have thrown themselves
at the feet of the older ones and convulsed with fear
and grief
and sadness...
feelings that only a child could truly know

the wound to their precious hearts must have cut deep
deeper than any medicine
or sweet comfort
or time
or love
could heal

I imagine that for days
and weeks
and months
and whole seasons that stretched into years
and decades
and generations that carried on into centuries
they must have painfully and anxiously waited for our return

they must have thought
– like children often do –
that at any moment we would 'round the path
 just outside their sleeping place
and their eyes would find themselves seeing us
and loving us
again

but we never came

and their longing must have carried them away from this misery
to another place
where old and lost hopes
expired dreams
cavernous despair
and tattered happiness
hang from dark and gloomy walls
like portraits of insanity
in a gallery of the suffering heart

their pain must have driven them to constant sadness
their sadness must have consumed all of their joy
and they must have found a more distant hiding place
and curled into small little knots of flesh
and slowly faded in spirit...
and in form...
and died ◈

The Story...Simply Told

there they stood...
hungry, dirty, tired and scared...
white folk gathered 'round
words were shouted back and forth...

there was great excitement

people were moving fast
wagons were brought up
chains were removed

new chains were applied

money exchanged hands...
there among the tears was lots of laughter

what a strange sight

death has never been so absurdly celebrated ◈

Chains On My Mind

chains on my body did not make me a slave
chains on my mind – did

whipping me did not make me a slave
whipping my children – did

making me toil like an animal in the blistering sun
did not make me a slave
watching my aged mother forced to work like a mule – did

making me wait on you hand and foot did not make me a slave
making my wife – with our child in her arms – suckle your child
while mine went hungry – did

telling me that I was less than human did not make me a slave
telling me I had no God – did

taking away my joy did not make me a slave
taking away my hope – did

telling me I would never know freedom did not make me a slave
believing you – did ◈

Hurry On Harriet

Harriet's coming to set me free
she won't leave me stranded by this tree
they said she'd come at half past three
so hurry on Harriet – hurry on!

I'm out here 'cuz I'm told she'd come
and tonight I'm not the only one
I got my wife my ma and my little son
please hurry on Harriet – hurry on!

I been beat down and near done in
I've lost it all septin' kin
and I'm 'fraid they'll be gone with the evenin' wind
Lord hurry on Harriet – hurry on!

I wadn't meant to be no slave
freedom's hope is too much to crave
I know my soul's enough to save
so hurry on Harriet – hurry on!

I've come as far as hope will go
my legs are weak...I'm getting slow
my heart's beating to and fro'
Jesus Harriet – hurry on!

This time tomorrow I'll be near freedomland
if sister Harriet's got me in her plan
I think I see her...
yes...
I can
over here Harriet – Lord let's hurry on! ◈

Easter Got Away

go on girl
go on
run right away
run for your natural life
run for all of us
run right into freedomland

You see Easter got away

the dispatch said something about she was the property of
so and so
and she was wanted back
there was even reward money put up
makes you think Easter was either awfully missed
or them chains they had on her weren't as strong as they were
'spose to be

So Easter got away

you know them old Africans said Easter wadn't never no slave no
how
they said that girl was born with the *juju* in her
she had visions they said
always dreamin' and talkin' 'bout being free

Yeah Easter got away

so she picked a sunny day
a day befitting her glorious ascension
got all scrubbed clean
put on her best frock
laced her boots all the way up

and strode right into Harriet's waiting arms.

Glory!

damn that Easter – they must have said!

But Easter got away

so go on girl
run all the way to freedomland
we're right behind you
those of us with the *juju* in us
those of us who are still always dreaming and talking 'bout being free ◈

What Was Done

hold a butterfly by its wings
and keep it from dancing from flower bowl to
sunny sky
it will one day not fly

steal a fragrant flower on a morning's walk
so that you might drink its colors in
it will bless you with its beauty-real
then wither from within

lock a sparrow in a cage
and hush its morning song
it will over time forget how to fly
grounded by this wrong

chain a people proud and full of natural love
to a senseless hate
and they will die a million deaths
redemption will come too late

and tell the gods that what was done was right
and that history tells but lies
they will not countenance your deceit
for the truth will rest forever in our timeless cries ◈

Brown Blossoms

brown blossoms from a single tree
strewn across an endless sea
oh how much you mean to me
...alone in this cold world

brown blossoms crying as they tumble down
loosed by pain and pulled to the ground
theirs is such an anguished sound
...alone in this cold world

brown blossoms scattered by the wind
never knowing home again?
forever savaged by this sin?
...alone in this cold world?

but...

brown blossoms bud anew each spring
and like feathers from a peace dove's wing
love is the branch to which they cling
blooming hope in a cold, cold world ❖

New Home

...rebirth / rethink / refeel

Like rich seed cast upon hard ground, we have pushed our roots into the soil of this nation. We've struggled and we've triumphed. We've known searing sorrow and tremendous joy. This land has become our home...

The Marcus Garvey Steamship Line

picking cotton for the man
running scared from the hooded klan
this whole damn thing is more than I can stan'
Lord take me outta here

pouring steel from day to night
washing floors in shoes too tight
working for nothin' sho' ain't right
Lord take me outta here

getting fed from the kitchen door
livin' hard and stayin' poor
boot kicks and blackjacks make me sore
lord take me outta here

decades fall – time movin' fast
Malcolm and Martin – didn't last
lost in the present – stuck in the past
lord take me outta here

and when you come lord – when it's my time
I'll gladly pack what little's mine
and load it up for that last climb
take me to heaven on the Garvey Steamship line ❖

The Great Migration

my daddy told me that when he was 16
he cried the cotton out of his soul
and just up and left *down south*
and headed for *up north* with all deliberate speed

...and somewhere between Selma and St. Louis
he became a man ◈

Harlem Circa 1926

the winter winds blew a scrap of newspaper up Lenox Avenue
as if it were playing a game
delivery men were already on their routes
the groceries were already fully stocked
and children
bundled no doubt by coddling moms
were draggin' their dreamy heads on to school

and great music was being born that morning on Lenox Avenue
and great words were being written
and great images were being painted
and sculpted
and turned
and choreographed

and great thoughts
about a people regal and free
were being conjured
and refined
and delivered to the open ears of a new-being

renaissance
renaissance
Black Renaissance
rebirth
rethink
refeel
relive
release

return

renaissance. ◈

Life In The City

just a little brown-skinned boy
sitting on a naked window sill
three flights up
eyes pointing out – not down
down
and he scrapes his eyes on the hard streets below
rough ground for such a young one
out
and his eyes can breath in a world that has some hope

just an old brown-skinned man
standing on a naked corner
three flights down
an amber bottle to steady him
an old lamp post to brace his arching back
eyes pointing up
not out
out there is where he met his pain
up
and his eyes can beg of God one more time
deliver me Lord...by and by

in an instance
the brown-skinned boy sees the old brown-skinned man
one looking
out
one looking
up
and in their gaze history is told
fates are sealed
...and life goes on in the city ◈

Come Sunday

the Right Reverend Booker W. Daniels was a God-fearing
no smoking
no joking
no dancing
no swearing
no staying out late
always in church
preachin' man

God called him from birth and he sho' let you know it!

he always opened church with
mornin' saints
and we were compelled by his deep basso-profundo voice
to offer
mornin' back
he'd start in from the beginning with how we was awful sinners
done-did-wrong-in-every-way-backsliders
and never-gonna-make-it-to-heaven-without-him
only-on-Sunday
pseudo-Christians!

we'd sit there like skint sheep
taking in his rebukes and lobbing back tired
amens
and watered down
hallelujahs
like Christian soldiers who done
surrendered long ago
and were just waiting for the line back home

he commanded up the choir like God must've bossed around the

thunder clouds.
and he would get out front of every song and bellow and blow
like a corked volcano.

grown women
little children
and even some of the men
would fall out and catch the spirit under the fire-and-brimstone of his
righteous Christian heat

then he'd set upon the deacons
to order up the stewards
to command the ushers
to go into every pocket and return with every claimed
and unclaimed dollar
even that last one you'd be saving for some sinful indulgence
you'd get on the way home from church.

then
there'd be some healing
drum playing
and more money collectin'
the reverend always saved plenty time for collectin'

and surely every Sunday,
the reverend would launch into his sermon 'bout why the Black man
was chosen by God to save the world
using only the shear force of love

the church would grow quiet
little babies would stop their wailing

the kids would stop their fidgeting in the pews
and we'd all just sit there in awe of our tremendous responsibility

Reverend Daniels would tell us that as saints
we were commissioned by God himself
to right this wicked world
and how if we just had a little more faith
and a little mo' Jesus
we'd glory in this God's work

well by then soft tears would be falling from every cheek
you'd get to feeling all warm and important inside
and the reverend would tell you how much he believed in you
and how much he prayed for your salvation
you'd sorta sit up a little straighter and hold your head up more
before long the healing of those words would've bored
deep into your human soul
glory!
glory hallelujah!

church would hardly be out 'fore you'd start wishing it was
Sunday all over again. ◈

Momma Pearl's Soul Food

even though the letters
once white and outlined in red
were nearly gone
it was still clear this was Pearl's Place
Momma Pearl's Place –
Fine food for fine Peoples

the aromatic evidence of Pearl's handiwork would capture you for
a block in every direction
bathe you in the sumptuousness of her kitchen
and bring you expectantly to her door

inside waiting – always – was Pearl
Momma Pearl
with her deep brown skin
cold black hair – only graying at the temples – and tied neatly under a
hair net
and a broad smile

Momma wore thick glasses
'cuz she couldn't see too good
and owing to that she called everyone that graced her kitchen
chile

come on in chile and have a seat
she'd say
what can Momma gets fo' ya now

Pearl was a week full of sweet brown candy
her love was fattening and she'd serve it up with generous
dollops of warm pats on the hand and wet full-lipped kisses
all over your cheek

in between the greens and cornbread
beans and rice
and chicken smothered in gravy
Momma Pearl would solve your problems
heal your wounds
and give you enough mother wit to find your way through life

Momma would make sure you knew 'fore you left outta her place
that you was loved
she'd batter you with
honeys and babies
and fry you in the genuine love of her soul

you always left Momma Pearl's fully fed
dining royally on a full-course meal of Momma's goodness.

Momma Pearl's was truly food for the soul. ◈

My Black Cocoon

I lived my entire childhood on 32nd street
in a white house
that had three small bedrooms
and a tiny kitchen

my house was surrounded on every side by
houses that looked just like it
and inside those houses were people
who looked just like me
they were my people
and we belonged to each other

and every day was the same as the day before
and we cried
and we laughed
and people died
and little ones were born
and the earth turned slowly on 32nd street

Mrs. Johnson who lived up the street
had too many children
Mr. Bill around the corner used to cut my hair
Mr. Rose the grocer lived up over the store with Mrs. Rose
who had bad feet
Mr. Parsons lived next door
he was a preacher
and Sugar – that's what he told everyone to call him –
never worked
but he had a fine car and lots of girlfriends

everyone knew my name
some of the old people just called me "sonnyboy"
I always called them "maam" and "sir"
I never spoke until spoken to
and I always looked grown folks in the eyes
when they spoke to me

my friends and I played all day in the summer
hated going to school in the winter
and seemed to grow closer with every season
we played together
fought together
and loved each other
without ever really saying the words

and as I grew
I knew I was special
'cuz I knew I was loved

and I think often now
about my Black cocoon. ◈

When I Met Elijah

brother passed me on the street one day
he sported a fine pin-striped suit on top of a seriously white shirt
and had on a bow tie that was tied so tight it looked like it
would decapitate him if he ran after me any faster

I told him
I wadn't having no paper – I ain't political

he begged for a minute anyhow
the Number 8 was late and it was hot
and I was too dog tired to shoo this persistent
pain-in-the-neck brother away

so I parked one tired ear on him and kept the other on the alert
for the Number 8
he must've told me 47 times that *Jesus was the white mans' God*
that Mohammed belonged to me
and that I had to get real about the state of things
...I had to open my eyes
...stop eating that pig
...drinking that white man's liquor

he must've went on with this over-practiced sermonette for an hour

where is the Number 8
how come white folks picked this one day to run on c.p. time
I thought

I'd stopped listening at about the time when he said
I had a "slave's mentality"
I shoulda stomped this signifying, sloganizing little brother's behind

and hailed a hack
and I was gonna when...

out of the clear blue he ups and tells me that *he loves me*
and that he would pray for me
and that he would welcome me at his mosque anytime

he calls me *king*
you know – *tells me that in Africa I was a king*
I wadn't born to be no slave
and he says that *I deserve to be treated like a hero for*
surviving in this racist country
and then he tells me that he's proud of me for hanging tough anyhow
he offers me a bean pie
I dig in my work pants for a dollar bill that emerges from my
pocket just as wrinkled and tired as I felt
he *thanks me*
says some Arabic shit I don't understand and moves on up the
street

and I was left with the heat
tired feet
no Number 8
...and a new feeling. ◈

Little Black Angels

little Black angels with sweet brown eyes...

jumping
and running
darting from here to there
lighting only like a butterfly does on an open morning glory

little Black angels with sweet brown eyes...

singing
and playing
laughing out smiles with deep dimples
the cadence of their gleeful sounds play like a symphony in my heart

little Black angels with sweet brown eyes...

fluttering
and
crying
tears that can break a heart or suspend a moment motionless
as they tumble
down their precious little faces

little Black angels with sweet brown eyes
quiet
and
sleeping
the rhythm of their breathing steady like the pendulum in an old
grandfather clock

little Black angels with sweet brown eyes...

questioning
and innocent
what is their place in this world?
what is their place in my soul?

little Black angels with sweet brown eyes...
see so much ◈

Old Sistah

old sistah
where are you going?
tell me now
what are you doing?
and with whom are you rushin' off to talk,
that's put so much trouble in your walk?

old sistah
every morning you push by my door
your gaze is fixed – your walk is sure
I know you've got some kinda' plan
you rushing off to meet some man?

old sistah
I see you roll by at night
your eyes look dim in the sunset light
your face looks drawn and your walk has slowed
you're moving hard cuz' your legs have bowed

well one day old sistah stopped to catch my stare
she asked
who are you to cause a care?
I replied
I want to know what you're all about
I spoke up quick and the words were out

so she spoke to me in a solemn way
for sister had no time for play
she said
sistah figured long ago
that in life you'd better have some place to go
it's what you do... not what you know

so each mornin' whether snow or rain
I walks down to where you catch the train
and I sits all day long inside the station
and watch these fools from every nation
then towards evenin' I head on back
and cross along my mornin' tracks
there's no meaning to this you might say
to waste so much good time this way

but some folks they gots jobs to do
and I guess old sistah's got hers too
to watch these fools and watch 'em right
and make it safely home at night

old sistah where are you going?
tell me now what are you doing?
and with whom are you rushing off to talk?
that's put so much trouble in your walk? ◈

Jazzzzzzzzzssss...

jazzzzzzzzzzsssssss.....

jazz is a voice that comes on low and smokey
it gets inside your head
and explodes into a million syncopated polyrythms
beating out an African groove **too damn old** to even name
so old and ancestral
you play it or you hear it 'cause you have to...
it's such a deep vibe

jazz is soul/heart/feet/hips and nodding of the head music
launching passion like a diving board
letting you jackknife into warm pools of sweet remembrances
the kind that brings on those summer smiles that just sit up
on your face awhile

jazz is my Black gift to the world
each note coiled around the things I've seen
the lives I've lived
the things I've lost
it's every Black thing I know

horns melt into piano strings like memories into dreams
a drum beat voices moody intentions
and all the while the bass is keeping it together and strong like
mother-love

thumm...thum...thuumm...deeda...doodoo...deedeeda...da da da
da da da da deeeee... daaaa...ssssss....dumm.....yeah! ◈

Brother's Got To Be On Time

I know time is a movin' now
we've all got things to do
people to be
roles to act out
I know that

I'm busy too!
I too
have planned too much life into this single moment

but please – please
let me take a minute now and notice those...
rich ebony eyes
that...curly-haired head
those...kissable, pillowy lips
that...generous nose
and that luv – ull – lee
night-to-day – and all the hours in between
skin

if you were a biscuit baby
I'd smother you with honey and sop you up!
hmmmmm...!!

but...
I ain't got time for that now
no no no no no...
I've got to run
your goodness and my appreciation of it is gonna hav'ta wait
that ain't gonna pay the bills baby...uh uh child

so give me a little sugar...
and pray I make it on time

what...
tell you what...

tell you once more about those pillowy
kissable lips?
child
you must be clean out your mind!
I've got to go!
brother's got to be on time! ◈

Am I?.... You Bet I Am

...and in case you think I'm not mad
that I have no anger
...that I'm over it
...that all is well
and I've moved on

...in case you thing there are no more tears
and curses
and swear words fiercely yelled
and epitaphs about you and your momma

...just in case you think that my fist aren't doubled up
and my heart isn't pounding a murderous beat
and my teeth aren't clinched
and the veins on my forehead
– you know the ones that only bulge out when I'm really mad –
aren't about to bust

...and just in case you haven't heard
that slavery wasn't really all that long ago
and race – ism
and class – ism
and sex – ism
and mine – ism
isn't truly dead

let me inform you...

come a little closer so I can give you the word
peep this:

I'M MAD!

I'M MAD!

I'M MAD!!! ◈

Keeping On

some mornings I awake with a single thought on my mind...
I must be something
really special
to have come through so much
and still have so much love left in my heart ◈

I'll Go

I will go home someday...

truth

the globe

and history

all bend back across themselves. ◈

My Home

...this Black skin is a blessing
great and good

My life, like all of our lives, has been shaped by the same forces that have defined our experience as children of the diaspora. Life has had it's grand moments, times of triumph, and it's moments of challenges and disappointment. But through it all, life has been rich and full of mystery...

Just Like A Child

I often thought as a little child
when I wasn't running/playing/joying loud
wouldn't it be wild
if when another child
who touched my Black skin out of curiosity
would become shaded Black just like me...
magically and instantaneously!

wouldn't he be surprised
I'd love to see the joy in his eyes...
'cuz surely then he'd have a chance to know
M'dear, Mr. Bill and Poppa Jo'
they too are hued in the same Black skin
so they'd love him lots and call him kin

they'd hold him close and rock and sing
about how he came from kings and queens
and how his people long ago
figured out what makes life so...
grand and beautiful

he'd have a chance to hear Billie and Coltrane and Miles
and he'd swing to a different rhythm and dance a funky style
and he'd talk in words that just made sense
and not be bothered by grammar or tense
'cuz he'd know it's in the feelings that love is shared
and no word or sound should ever be spared

and he'd know all about them brave ones that came before
those ancestor folk who opened doors
and let hope shine in on his beautiful Black skin

and put that pride deep within
his African soul

surely every child would want this gift I thought
something so precious it couldn't be bought
so in my child-heart reverie
I'd climb into the nearest tree
and wait till I saw a not-Black child
and descend on him like a panther cloud
and spread this gift on him head and toe
and soon that child would come know
what every Black child feels:

that this Black skin is a blessing
great and good
and is to be shared
like any special thing should

I thought this often as a child ◈

Black Madonna

(for Ruth)

this won't take long
this love poem to Black Madonna
true testaments of love don't require wasted words

let's just say she is everything to me
all the love
all the strength
and **the** constant source of universal and eternal wisdom

let me say she has a rare beauty
and counts God and Nature as her sisters
...she knows the natural order of things

I'll simply add that she is determined to raise this world
one Black child at a time
and she has raised me
far above what I had hoped to be ◈

Blues for A. Y.

I know the liquid in this bottle is not good for me
it won't lift my burden or make me free
it won't change the way the world does me

but it gets me through the night

I know it makes my hands shake a bit
and sometimes quake
but I got too much misery at stake
living life on the outside
for pretense sake

but it gets me through the night

I know I've lost – oh I've lost so
and through that door someday you'll go
and leave me sitting here on this floor

Lord get me through that night

And on this bed I'll lay me down
with a painful wince
a sigh
a frown
and consider how this damn drink done pulled
me 'round

just let me get through that night

And as I look back I hang my head
and curse this bottle and the death if fed
maybe one more drink and then it's said
I'm done

...let me go into the night ◈

Reprise for A.Y.

Black father
your goodness
lives
this day
still...

in
me ◈

Just The Facts

I am a Black man

let me say it again

I am a powerful man-force

let me say it again

I am a fully conscious – completely aware soul-being

let me say it again

I am the bearer of liberating truth

let me say it again

I am all love

Let me say it one more time

I am a Black man ◈

Am I Black Enuff?

Lord knows I don't want to open that book...
the Book of Pain

...I was told my skin was too damn light
yellow boy
half and half
white boy

...I was told my lips were not full enough
too flat
and therefore incapable of speaking Black
...too proper

...I was told my hair was
good
which was really bad
goodness and badness always seemed like such heavy terms
for something so un-important as hair

I was told
I was told
I was told

...and the tears come as I turn the heavy pages

how do you end such a book?

do you simply run out of breath
sigh
and be done with it?

do you rip out its pages

and burn its cover in the fires of constant shame?

or do you carefully put it down...
let it rest upon the nearby table
and from time to time
– when you need to heal –
open its pages once more? ◈

Love

(for Deborah)

...and what do I say of love?
do I say it is a fragrance to be worn to seduce
to tempt the feeble emotions that guard the soul?

do I say it is a ripple on a pretty pond
that echoes its message in succeeding replications
each moving further from the truth?

should I say it is a work of art
a visual treat with grace and balance and complication?

perhaps I would be better to speak of it as a cause or force
– spiritual and ethereal –
not bound by physical explanation or easy descriptions
tethered to simple ideas
and expressed within the limitations of mere language

no...I should say that love is a bitter thing –
it veils and enslaves
one cannot move so easily when one has been caught by love
acts because of love
or fails to act
for fear of it

I should say that love is painful
it brings suffering
agony
longing
desperation
the sickest of deaths

love heaps hurt on top of hurt

I must be sure to say that love makes it
really hard to think straight
it clouds up the mind
throws things off inside
and causes a lot of questioning

perhaps I should say all of that and no more
'cause love would demand too much be said about it
it would have you spend too much time on it
too much effort

...so I'll say only that love exists
it is wondrous, universal and beguiling
and nothing more...

nothing more...

nothing more...for now ◈

What's Inside

they say nothing's hotter than the sun
and that when stars die, their pain is so bitter
they burn a hole in the evening sky

they say nothing's hotter than Black rage
and that when Black boys die, their pain is so bitter
they burn a hole in our hearts

before today
they used to say nothing was hotter
than the sun ◈

Somewhere Between Martin And Malcolm

martin had a dream
and i got to bed early so i could dream it too
but then i remembered the insomnia that started in Memphis
so i never got to sleep

malcolm said do it by any means necessary
so i went out and got a gun
but i never loaded it
maybe it wasn't necessary after all

and here i sit
somewhere between martin and malcolm
knowing i should do something
and hoping i don't have to

'cause if i got to love
and turn the other cheek
i may not have enough face to
keep my cool

and if i got to burn down
to build up
i may not be able to put out the fire

so...

here i sit
somewhere between martin and malcolm
knowing i should do something
and praying
all the while
i don't have to ◆

A Little Inspiration

(for my son Brandon)

sitting here on daddy's lap
love in small delicate eyes
looking out and through me

this is my son this night
lights out but one
at the old desk where I write

he is close and warm
and moves slowly
with all of the grace
that carefree loves allows

holding him now in my arms
feeling his warm little cheek on mine
kissing his tiny, knowing little hands...

candles may flicker in the church tonight
and robins may take flight
subtle is the wind that blows through my life
blowing in now
this small baby boy ◈

Rainbow

(for my son Ryan)

one night
it was storming hard and loud
outside
around
and through
our house

lightening jolted us into fear
raindrops made loud explosions
as they threw themselves against the window panes
and the lights flickered –
threatening at any moment
to surrender us to the darkness of the storm

it was at that moment that my little one
through all of his tears
held my hand
found my eyes
and said an urgent prayer out loud:

God please send us a rainbow

at that very moment the storm halted dead in its tracks
the sky put away its frightening face
and the clouds folded themselves into little puffs
of grey and white
and slowly
but boldly
a rare and intense rainbow unfurled across the sky

it was then that I first knew that my youngest child
was an angel
and that God had sent me a rainbow in him

...and from that moment on
I have celebrated the colors of his love ◈

Just A Little Poem For Me

some poems don't
    some poems won't
        some poems can't

but this poem does...

make me smile ◈

Held Tears On A Grey Morning

when life is lived well
there is a certain pattern to it
the colors all match the sky
the sky is always blue
and love fills the nostrils like fragrant flowers
wearing the morning's dew

when life is lived well
there's a groove
a beat
symbols melt behind the drums
piano strings ride upon a steady bass
and passion leaps from the soul without hesitation

when life is truly lived well
hands glide easily into fur-lined gloves
as if riding a fine bead of oil

rain water rolls neatly from the brim of a wide hat
tumbling into drops
drops into spoonfuls
and spoonfuls descend like cascades
making full puddles on the ground
that wash away any uncertainties in your step

...but this morning
there is a certain melancholy in me
brown face resting on browner hands
elbows pushed into the thighs
weight brought forward as if to rush from this place...

life goes well
then sometimes...
my eyes well up as if ready to yield a tear to
my melancholy grey morning
but...it holds at the corner
and thus a waterfall is quieted
stilled
...and put away
saved for yet another time.

when life is lived well
tears are held on a grey morning ◈